THE GRIZZLY GAZETTE

by Stuart J. Murphy · illustrated by Steve Björkman

shers

LEVEL
3

To Edna and Larry—and their troop of happy Ter Molen campers
—S.J.M.

The publisher and author would like to thank teachers Patricia Chase, Phyllis Goldman,
and Patrick Hopfensperger for their help in making the math in MathStart just right for kids.

HarperCollins®, ♣®, and MathStart® are registered trademarks of HarperCollins Publishers.
For more information about the MathStart series, write to
HarperCollins Children's Books, 1350 Avenue of the Americas, New York, NY 10019,
or visit our website at www.mathstartbooks.com.

Bugs incorporated in the MathStart series design were painted by Jon Buller.

The Grizzly Gazette
Text copyright © 2003 by Stuart J. Murphy
Illustrations copyright © 2003 by Steve Björkman

Library of Congress Cataloging-in-Publication Data
Murphy, Stuart J.
   The grizzly gazette / by Stuart J. Murphy ; illustrated by Steve Björkman.
      p.   cm. — (MathStart)
   "Percentages. Level 2."
   ISBN 0-06-000027-9 — ISBN 0-06-000025-2 (lib. bdg.) — ISBN 0-06-000026-0 (pbk.)
   1. Percentage—Juvenile literature. [1. Percentage.] I. Björkman, Steve, ill. II. Title. III. Series.
QA117 .M874 2003   2001024633
513.2'4—dc21

Typography by Elynn Cohen

1   2   3   4   5   6   7   8   9   10

First Edition

"I'd love to do it," said Corey. "Do you really think I could win?"

It was Tuesday of the last week at Camp Grizzly. On Saturday everyone would vote for the camp mascot. If Corey won, she would get to wear the famous Grizzly Bear costume and lead all 100 campers in the Grizzly Parade. And her photo would be displayed forever in the Grizzly Bear Hall of Fame.

"Sure you can win!" said Jacob.

"I've love to be the Grizzly Bear, but Daniel and Sophie have already started their campaigns," said Corey.

"Daniel is really popular," Corey added, "and Sophie belongs to the Boat Club. That's the biggest club at camp. Look at this article in *The Grizzly Gazette*."

There was a poll in *The Grizzly Gazette*. The reporters wanted to see who was ahead. They asked all 100 campers how they planned to vote.

Then they printed a circle graph to show how all, or 100%, of the campers felt.

"Don't worry," said Jacob. "We haven't even started yet."

"Yeah," said Katie. "Look at all those undecided votes. You still have a chance."

"Okay," said Corey. "I'll do my best."

THE GRIZZLY GAZETTE

SOPHIE AND DANIEL NECK AND NECK

25 said they would vote for Sophie

25 said they would vote for Daniel

25% 25%

50%

50 Hadn't made up their minds

On Wednesday, Corey announced that she was entering the race. Late that afternoon, *The Grizzly Gazette* ran another poll. Again they asked the 100 campers how they planned to vote.

"We've got a long way to go," said Corey later that afternoon.

"But we're just getting started," said Jacob.

"You already have 10% of the vote," said Katie. "In just one day!"

15

On Thursday, Daniel had flyers delivered to every camper. The Boat Club wore T-shirts with Sophie's name on them.

Corey went around to all the cabins. She said hi to everybody. And she asked people what they would really like the mascot to do in the parade.

On Friday the *Gazette* printed one last poll.

"You've got more than 20%," said Katie.

"You're gaining on them!" said Jacob.

THE GRIZZLY GAZETTE

SOPHIE HOLDS THE LEAD

36 said they would vote for Sophie

28 said they would vote for Daniel

21 said they would vote for Corey

15 hadn't made up their minds

36%
28%
21%
15%

75% of camp rabbits would rather have carrot cake than chocolate shakes

On Saturday, Daniel gave out candy bars. The Boat Club held a regatta for Sophie. And at the campfire that night, each candidate got a chance to make a speech.

"Vote for me!" said Sophie. "I can lead the parade in style!" And she did a cartwheel right in front of everybody.

"Vote for me!" said Daniel. "Remember the candy bars!"

Then it was Corey's turn.

21

Corey stood up. She was a little nervous, but she spoke clearly. "I asked a lot of you what you wanted the mascot to do in the parade," she said. "And after I heard what you said, I decided to write a new camp cheer."

"Huh?" said Daniel.

"Who cares about a cheer?" said Sophie.

All the members of the Music Club stood up and started playing their instruments. And Corey sang the new Grizzly cheer.

"1, 2, 3, 4—
Listen to our Grizzly roar!
Grrrr, grrrr, grrrr!"

The Music Club began marching around the campfire. One by one, the campers jumped up and got in line. Corey sang some more.

"2, 4, 6, 8—

The Grizzly Bears are really great!

Grrrr, grrrr, grrrr!"

Soon everyone was marching and singing along.

The election was Sunday. *The Grizzly Gazette* published a special edition as soon as the votes were counted.

Later that day, Corey put on her costume, gave big bear-hugs to Jacob and Katie, marched to the front of the line, and led the whole camp—all 100%—in singing the new Grizzly cheer.

"1, 2, 3, 4—
Listen to our Grizzly roar!
Grrrr, grrrr, grrrr!
2, 4, 6, 8—
The Grizzly Bears are really great!
Grrrr, grrrr, grrrr!
The Grizzly Bears. The Grizzly Bears.
THAT'S US!"

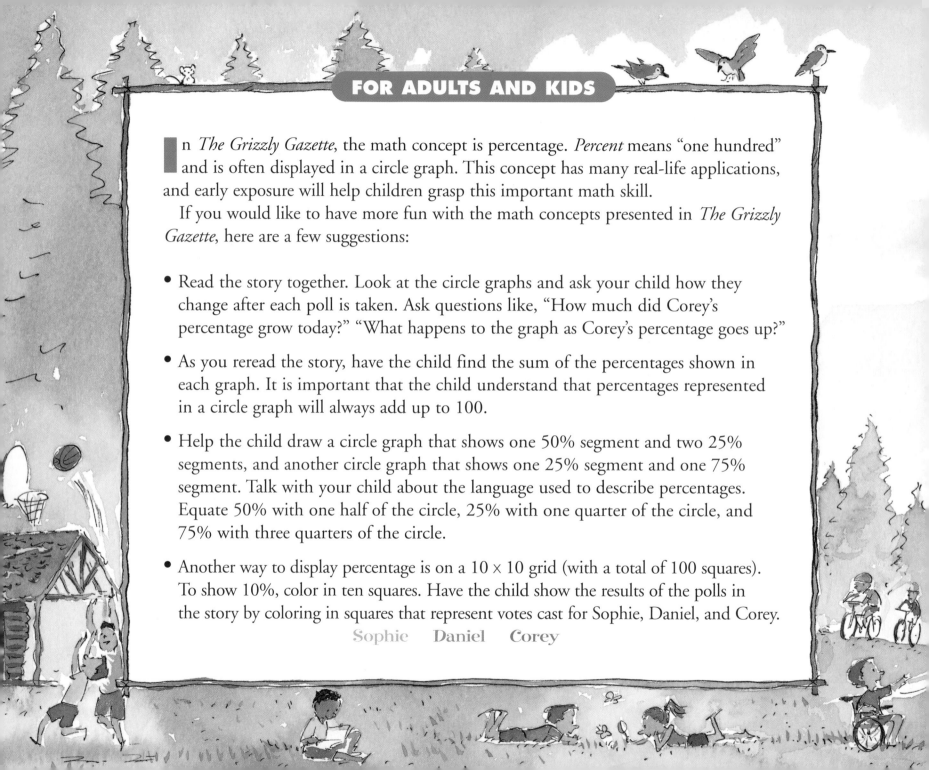

In *The Grizzly Gazette*, the math concept is percentage. *Percent* means "one hundred" and is often displayed in a circle graph. This concept has many real-life applications, and early exposure will help children grasp this important math skill.

If you would like to have more fun with the math concepts presented in *The Grizzly Gazette*, here are a few suggestions:

• Read the story together. Look at the circle graphs and ask your child how they change after each poll is taken. Ask questions like, "How much did Corey's percentage grow today?" "What happens to the graph as Corey's percentage goes up?"

• As you reread the story, have the child find the sum of the percentages shown in each graph. It is important that the child understand that percentages represented in a circle graph will always add up to 100.

• Help the child draw a circle graph that shows one 50% segment and two 25% segments, and another circle graph that shows one 25% segment and one 75% segment. Talk with your child about the language used to describe percentages. Equate 50% with one half of the circle, 25% with one quarter of the circle, and 75% with three quarters of the circle.

• Another way to display percentage is on a 10 × 10 grid (with a total of 100 squares). To show 10%, color in ten squares. Have the child show the results of the polls in the story by coloring in squares that represent votes cast for Sophie, Daniel, and Corey.

Sophie   Daniel   Corey

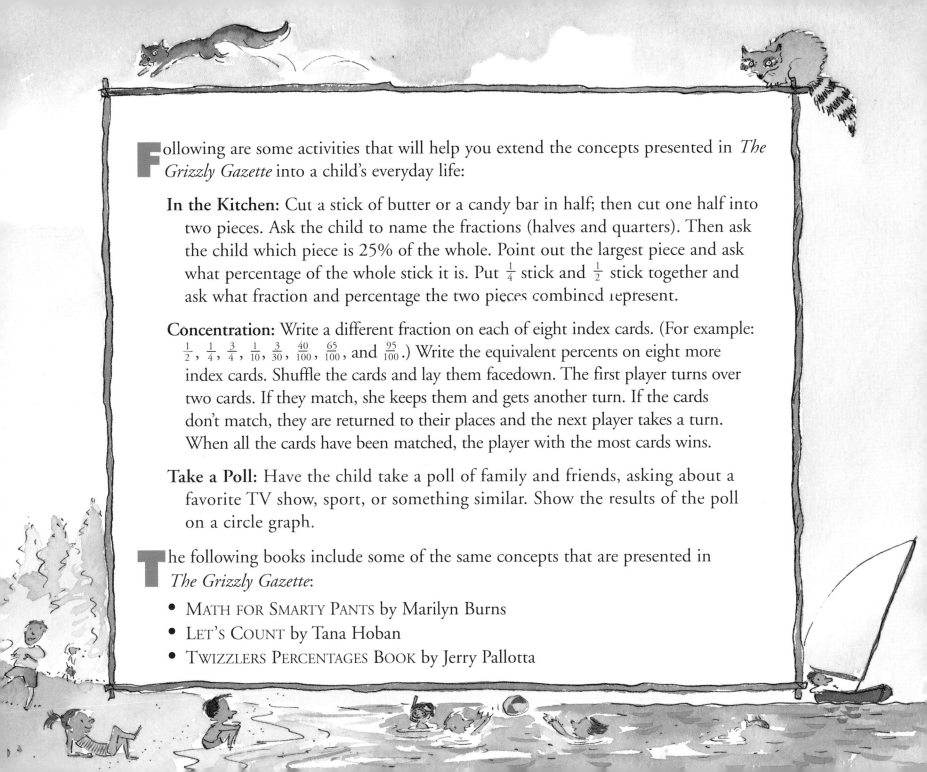

Following are some activities that will help you extend the concepts presented in *The Grizzly Gazette* into a child's everyday life:

In the Kitchen: Cut a stick of butter or a candy bar in half; then cut one half into two pieces. Ask the child to name the fractions (halves and quarters). Then ask the child which piece is 25% of the whole. Point out the largest piece and ask what percentage of the whole stick it is. Put $\frac{1}{4}$ stick and $\frac{1}{2}$ stick together and ask what fraction and percentage the two pieces combined represent.

Concentration: Write a different fraction on each of eight index cards. (For example: $\frac{1}{2}$, $\frac{1}{4}$, $\frac{3}{4}$, $\frac{1}{10}$, $\frac{3}{30}$, $\frac{40}{100}$, $\frac{65}{100}$, and $\frac{95}{100}$.) Write the equivalent percents on eight more index cards. Shuffle the cards and lay them facedown. The first player turns over two cards. If they match, she keeps them and gets another turn. If the cards don't match, they are returned to their places and the next player takes a turn. When all the cards have been matched, the player with the most cards wins.

Take a Poll: Have the child take a poll of family and friends, asking about a favorite TV show, sport, or something similar. Show the results of the poll on a circle graph.

The following books include some of the same concepts that are presented in *The Grizzly Gazette*:

- MATH FOR SMARTY PANTS by Marilyn Burns
- LET'S COUNT by Tana Hoban
- TWIZZLERS PERCENTAGES BOOK by Jerry Pallotta